The MissedPrint of
a Poet

The MissedPrint of a Poet

jus Will

© 2015 by jus Will.   All rights reserved.

Published by Vantage Point Publishing
Indianapolis, IN 46218

No part of this publication may be reproduced or transmitted in any form or by any means, electronic or mechanical, including photocopy, or any information storage and retrieval system, without permission from the publisher. The only exception is a brief quotation in printed reviews.

Limit of Liability/Disclaimer of Warranty: While the publisher and author have used their best efforts in preparing this book, they make no representations or warranties with respect to the accuracy or completeness of the contents of this book and specifically disclaim any implied warranties of merchantability or facilities for a particular purpose. No warranty may be created or extended by any persons. The advice or strategies herein may not be suitable for your situation. You should consult with a professional where appropriate. Neither the publisher nor author should be liable for any loss of profit or any other incidental damages, including but not limited to special, consequential, or other damages.

This is a work of fiction. Names, characters, businesses, places, events and incidents are either the products of the author's imagination or used in a fictitious manner. Any resemblance to actual persons, living or dead, or actual events is purely coincidental.

ISBN 978-0-9883939-9-8

The publisher would appreciate notification where errors occur so that they may be corrected in subsequent printing and/or editions. Please send comments to the publisher by emailing to biz@amorousink.com

Printed in the United States of America

Dedication

This book is dedicated to my parents, Will and Val King, whom have genetically infused my DNA with artistic abilities beyond my own comprehension.

To Kesha Williams for showing me what positivity, commitment, and drive are supposed to look like even from the passenger's seat. To the incredible Tasha Jones (poet) ,for loving our city and our craft, with a passion that's not measurable.

This book is dedicated to the great ones, M'reld Green, Red Storm, Saul Williams, LEMON, & my adopted uncle Kwabena Dinizulu, to name a few. To my private investor, you have made this book possible.

This book is dedicated to my sister, Terri Montgomery and my nephew Marlan King for those early morning and late night calls while I read my latest piece.

To the gone but not forgotten Queen B. LOVE YOU QUEEN!

To my family that's related and those that were selected. To The 3 Kings (Ania, Quiarra, and Will IV), and X Man (Xavier King). I love you 4 beautiful children of mine. To my teammates, past and present, Brittany, Monique, Ambur, DeNyne, Tony, Michelle, Adrian, StacE', The Greer's, Frank, Mason, Kenyatta, Nyra, and Lena. Brittany and Monique . . . PERKINS?

To anyone that has and/or continues to support my journey. If I forgot you please blame my head and not my heart. I'M OLD! This book is dedicated to YOU! Remember to "BUILD a poem & WRITE an empire" . . . Enjoy

x

jus Will's Dictionary

While reading his thoughts that spill to paper, he puts his own twist on common words. Do not be offended as he is not and intended for the words to be spelled just as they are.

Couse – cause-because

Coochie-speaks for itself

Blockin'

Feed'em

Doin'

Aint

Tellin'

Sho' aint

To've

Pushin'

Auditorical

Freaknicity

These are just a few that you will encounter. They are just as they are supposed to be. Enjoy!

QUEEN MOTHER

The strength to man comes from within the soil that held the seed
To love and cherish this womanhood and supply her every need
Mother, is an understatement that describes the triumphs I've seen
You've accomplished more with yourself and your kids and through this I label you

QUEEN

CONGRATULATIONS

My nephew's getting married soon
    You growing up man, this shit is GREAT
No more concern about you got burned
    Or which piece of bad coochie you just ate
I know some of these brothers don't have a clue
    A few just can't relate
As to how you givin' up these notches and stuff
    But it's a new life you're about to create
Them playa days was fun now they're over and done
    No more hoes for everyday of the week
But the good thing is this, it aint shit that you'll miss
    couse your whole life you done been a damn freak
And though I say it with a smile, it's some serious shit
    So pay attention to what I'm mentioning here
Not to frighten or Sca that I wouldn't dare
    Just to put a small bug in your ear
So good luck on your travels even when it unravels
    Stay strong couse it'll be okay
And when you're stressed and must talk just remember
I've walked on your path the exact same way
Know that life will be good as we all knew it would

       couse you've earned everything that
you own
And with blessings you've gotten at times
spoiled rotten
       From this day on you'll never be alone

DEAR SISTERS

Dear sister although we sometimes fight
        you always manage to make my days bright
You never ran when things got rough
        and though no man is good enough
I hope your marriage can only grow
        Congratulations ... your little bro

Dear sister you've always been so strong
        you continue to show me right from wrong
Although sometimes I stray away
        you always track me down to say
Never hold my head so low
        So thank you from ... your little bro

THESE 3 WORDS

I never imagined in my brightest thought
    that one day I would somehow say
The way that I feel is way too real
    and in scripture I shall display
I could TELL you I want you
I could SAY I need you
    but a pen best expresses my thoughts
Trapped by your essence addicted to your presence
    In your soul my rapture has been caught
Entangled by conversation
the sensation I feel is true bliss
    captivated by your spirit
and for that I write you this:

        I LOVE YOU

NO LEXUS (STUDIO PLAYER PT. 2)

IS MY GAME TOO LAME
        IS MY RAP JUST CRAP
TELL ME GIRL CAUSE I DESERVE TO KNOW
DO MY SKILLS GOT FRILLS
        IS MY VOICE NOT CHOICE
IS MY COLLAR TOO BLUE OR WON'T NO COLLAR DO
        TILL I RID MYSELF OF THIS PINTO
I'VE BEEN AROUND THE WORLD IN 80 DAYS
I GET FROM POINT A TO POINT B
BUT NONE THE LESS IT'S NO LS, NO GS, AND NO SC
I DON'T GOT NO MERCEDES
        ALDO DON'T GOT NO LADIES
NO VETTE, NO JAG, NO SUV
NO SWITCHES, NO BITCHES
NO BEATS, NO FREAKS
JUS' MY PINTO AND LITTLE O' ME
I CONTEMPLATE AND HESITATE AND SEE
        THE DRIVERS SEAT IN WHICH YOU SIT
YET I CRAM TO UNDERSTAND
        WHY I CAN'T BE YOUR MAN
AND YOU DRIVIN' YOUR MOMMA'S SHIT

I STILL HATE HER

Hey Homie,
        You remember that broad that I told you about
I told her to leave and she still won't get out
Player hatin' on everybody that calls my crib
Makin' sure I ain't datin', I don't even know where she lives
She be sneakin' up on me like the butler on MR. DEEDS
hidin' in the bushes and jumpin' out from behind trees
I thought she was leavin', I guess I was wrong
that girl's so damn deceivin', she just keeps stringing me along
she's so full of crap, I aint never seen nothin' like this in my life
but this is the same chic, that told me to marry my wife
IS YOU IS, OR IS YOU AINT, MY BABY, maybe it's all a trick
I guess the answer is IS YOU AINT, couse you still makin' me sick
and as soon as I think I've got her out my system, she's right back in my brain
harrasin' my ass and got me actin' against the grain
This aint me, I's a playa' from the Himalayaz
Well...the hoosier state
soon as she see me with a honey she bein' funny
NIGGA WHO'S YOUR DATE!!

and my dumb ass keep on explainin',
this chic is awfully clever
always on my mind and I'm fillin' like she's been around forever
she's actually the reason I can't get close to nobody else, always playin' these freakin' games
Well, I'm tryin' to warn you about this girl, but I better whisper her name
Her name is Love, yeah playa' you already know
I hate Love, boy I still hate Love, but I still hate to see her go

I DO

Although my body's locked away
      my heart escapes these walls to say
that we will reunite in time
      your mountain of pleasure I soon shall climb
And when I reach the top we'll be together for eternity

HOW DO I KNOW

How do I know if I love you so?
        Could it be by the way I think?
I hear your voice when you're not there
        or see your reflection in my drink

How do I know if I love you so?
        One way that I can tell
Is the way my boat goes out afloat
        As your breath is like a breeze to my sail

How do I know if I love you so?
        When you're near, the way that my heart pounds
Plus the fact that I'm writing you this ... as silly as it may sound

Untitled

How can you not feel
    the way which I do
How can you not tell
    How you make me feel
Yes, the way I feel, think, and do
    Is because of your importance in my life
It is also my importance in life itself
My purpose is clearly seen
    Through the eyes of an angel and
reflected on the pool of purpose
    To be viewed by the masses as
all that is right in a man, a husband and a father
I'm telling you, that life is good
I'm telling you, that love is good
I'm telling you, that ...
you will succumb to the joy that I have to offer

    Thank you
      In Advance

10 REASONS WHY I LOVE YOU

Time and time again you ask why I love you so
Well here's a list to answer this, and from this day on you'll know

1. I love your energy, as positive as it may be
2. Your beauty, inside and out, for everyone to see
3. The way you make me laugh, even when I feel to cry
4. Your independence, is another reason why
5. Is the unselfishness that dwells within; your heart
6. I'm just as blissed today, as you made me from the start
7. Is simple, you're absolute, when it comes to sophistication
8. Your versatility, to handle each situation
9. You're always on my mind wishing that you were here
10. In case someone is reading this, I'll say it in your ear

NO LIMITS

No limits exist when it comes to this
    No boundaries, no rules, no laws
No hesitation, premeditation causes ejaculation
    With the taste of your edible draws

No guidelines to follow, eject and I'll swallow
    All pride has been laid to the side
Couse we doin' shit that's new and shit at least
To us cause it's stuff we aint tried

From your toes to your brow as long as you smile
You can moan, you can yell, you can scream,
    I can tell you that you fell in this daze once more
From the porch, to the couch, to the stool, on the car, on the bench, in the bed, and
quite often it's done on the floor

Your reflection, my erection, the affection is immense as you convince me that your satisfied all the way around
From your breast, I caress, down your backside
I glide as I travel the road to downtown

You ask the extend on how far we went, you
Can tell there are none we can't pass
No limits exist when it comes to this
Hell, I even have tasted your ass.

JUST US

HUG ME
  HIT ME
DATE ME
  HATE ME
KISS ME
  KICK ME
CUSS

HOLD ME
  SCOLD ME
TOUCH ME
  PUNCH ME
LIKE ME
  STRIKE ME
FUSS

LOVE YOU
  BUG YOU
TREAT YOU
  BEAT YOU
LAUGH WITH YOU
  LAUGH AT YOU
TRUST

NEED YOU
  FLEE YOU
CALL YOU
  APPALL YOU
REWARD YOU
  DISREGARD YOU

    THERE'S NO YOU OR ME

JUST US

MUSIC

Music is the essence of a world
    That's complete
It's universal, melodic, spiritual, acute, and chronic
Snaps, Claps, Raps, adapts to tight beats
Not tight in the snug sense
That's nonsense
Music has no past tense, pre-tense, or post-tense
The actuality is it relives Most Tense
Situations, Moods, Mind States, Closed Minds, Closed Gates and most make
Beautiful tunes, lovely tones, serene sounds
    But the profound pounds
Of bodies combined, entwined, unwind to replay
Music is the night, Music is the day
Music is the way the Earth is front state
    for this unwritten play
You never knew the true value of your part
Act 1 has just begun, Part 2 will never start
So focus on each clue, for this play is not an act
And listen to each note
Enhanced
Life's Soundtrack

NOW ALWAYS, FOREVER

Now niece by law

Always niece by love

Forever niece by life

HORNY

Day after Day after Day after Day
    Naked I rest in bed
Wondering is it that sleep comes last
    and I cum first instead
Of course the course of the intercourse train
    veers swiftly to my right
to dodge the fate I hoped would fall
    but drowsiness wins tonight
        But tomorrow will be different,
I'm convincing myself, while self says, "BE FOR REAL,"
Is my diddle too little, I'm confused by this riddle
And my weenie wants to know the damn deal
If it don't get right soon, I'm for certain to bust like a balloon in spiked room and my love is transforming to lust

    I'm Horny

A LITTLE NAP (HUSBAND'S ANTHEM)

ALL YOU NEED IS A LITTLE NAP
      I'VE HEARD THAT THRICE BEFORE
AND WHEN I LAY DOWN NEXT TO YOU
      I'M GREETED WITH A SNORE
I WAKE YOU, WE TALK, YOUR EYES CLOSE TIGHT
      AND YOU'RE RIGHT BACK TO YOUR Z'S
FORGETTING THE FUCKING TALKING THAT WE HAD
      LIKE YOU'VE GOT ALZHEIMER'S DISEASE
SO TO MY SPOT I RETURN AGAIN,
      DOING WHAT I DO WELL
WHO NEEDS SOME ASS WITH A GRIP LIKE THIS
      I GUESS COOCHIE CAN GO TO HELL
COUSE ALL YOU NEED IS A LITTLE NAP
      AT LEAST THAT'S WHAT YOU SAY
TONIGHT IS NO DIFFERENT, I KNEW THAT THIS MORNING
            IT'S JUST LIKE YESTERDAY

MARRIAGE

Marriage is a promise to sacrifice,
    forever and a few days past
To give away everything you have ever worked for
    even the shadow your silhouette once cast
It's a growth and a development
    The essence and the element
That combines two halves to make them whole
It's before the eyes of God, friends, and family
    and adds a fullness to the soul
Some call it fate or destiny
    others say it must be God's will
I dare not give it a name at all
But believe when I say that it's real
And although to make it work
you give your last, Just believe and
you'll fully receive
to be where these two have arrived today
takes a lifetime of love to achieve

DEDICATED TO MARLAN AND TASHA KING

MY SEED

Take Heed
The seeds been planted deep
Now I nurture so it might grow
To be
A tree as tall as me
And tower over those
Those who know the wrongs and rights
And still bloom a crooked fate
While you take light
And make a life
And sprout
Narrow and straight

I CONFESS

When emptiness feels my heart within
    And my soul can barely provide
I think of you and dreams come true
    That leave me teary eyed
From happiness and joy that's felt
    Each moment that we possess
I miss you dear with all my heart
    This Loneliness
    I CONFESS

As days go past and seem to last
    eternity and more
I realize it's no other one
    it is you that I adore
When it seems to be it's only me
    up against the world
It's good to know your actions show
    that you are still my girl

When obstacles lay in my path
    and barriers stand tall
Sometimes I slip or lose my grip
    but you still catch my fall
And days when I'm in misery
    and cannot give my best
I thank you for getting me through those times
    My Love, Dear
    I CONFESS

TO MAKE YOU STAY

I would pay to make you stay
    if I would still feel this way
    but the truth is
Money can't supply my emotions
Money is a tool, demanded by fools
    and true love flows wild like an ocean
A sea of happiness in which one swims
    an all-natural body with finite rivers and streams
As I bathe in your waters the tide quickly rises
    My physical quivers
And my mental continues its dreams
My disillusioned psyche premeditates the
    thought of your intimate touch
I've dismissed many things and made many changes,
    but never missed a being this much
If I told you I missed you a billion and one,
    then multiply that by the days in a week
And you'll get a tenth of a fraction of the true satisfaction
    that I get every time that we speak
So I seek to find a way
    to make my days turn blue from gray
And in my mind I make the time stand still
So when you return
I'm sure we've both learned
That a love this intense
Is
    For Real

UNTITLED

All that I want from you is ...
        EVERYTHING
See, I'm really not asking for much
Your body, your soul, your freedom,
your mind, and periodically, I need your touch
I'm not a greedy man I can handle the crumbs
The remains of what's left is enough
Sometimes when I think of you saying
I DO
I think you were just calling my bluff
I think you were just calling my bluff
I think you were just calling my bluff
Testing to see where I stood
Never to fathom, imagine, consider, to think
truly my love could be good

THIS YEAR

It's the end of the year 2000 and 3
       and all roads are clear, I'm hopin', for me
I'm startin' a new life, as well as I can
       focused on bein' a much better man
and although this year really wasn't half bad
       I've been workin' real hard, and been a hell of a dad
but now is my time to really buckle down
       I'm writing my book plus I'm spiritually sound
and I aint all off into that religious B.S.
       just doin' what's right and tryin' my best
I'm aimin' on my home, my career, and my kids
       and forgiving these devils for the deeds that they did
I'm relinquishing the negative, it exists no more
and this will be my year
       2004

THIS SHIT AINT POETRY

This shit aint poetry
       Nigga this is real life
              The strain the pain, the drama, the rain
           The good and bad
The baby momma, and the baby momma other baby dad
This shit aint poetry, nigga this is real ... life
The bad ass kids, the bad relationships, the bad in a good way, coochie, and my bad ass situation with my estranged wife
This shit aint poetry
       This is day to day, every day, every way, shape or form
This tight shit is sometimes
This bullshit ... is the norm
This shit aint poetry
This is racism, escapism, slavery, freedom, understanding and confusion
This is the crap that you see, thought you seen,
       Would like to see, rather it be real or illusion
This shit aint poetry,
       It's crack addicts, hustlers, and those that fall in between...
You know what I mean
       This is street shit ... grimy and gritty penitentiary thoughts, and that broad with the big ass titties
           This is the Nubian queen shit
                  The rest in peace shit

The never been seen shit
The ... to say the least shit
This is gay, straight, love and hate
Destiny and fate, plus divine intervention
This is, police shot a nigga in the back and get
Pay with a lame ass suspension
SHIT
This shit aint poetry
This is ... my daddy used to beat me
My boyfriend won't eat me
My girlfriend mistreats me
The niggas at the crap house cheat me
This is pimp shit and hoe shit
Weed shit and blow shit
My daughter is too fast ... but my bitch, is too slow shit
This is Michael Jackson, before, during, and since he's been weird
Real nose, fake nose, whose nose, his shit's disappeared
This is hip hop, r and b, jazz, rock, and blues
This is 3 piece suits, and cowboy boots
Now and later gators, throw backs with matching shoes
(STOMPING IN MY AIR FORCE ONES)
This is my wheels still spinnin' shit
This is rollin' on twenty fo's
This is broke ass nigga shit
High school hoopin' shit, crossin' 'em over

    Skippin' college goin' to the pros
This is that real shit
    This is that Aretha Franklin
      This is Floetry
This is Big Daddy Kane, and Lil' Wayne
   And Luther Vandross
       But ... this shit aint poetry
         This shit aint poetry

IN 2003

GIRLS, WOMEN, LADIES, DAMES, BROADS, CHICS, FREAKS, HONEYS, BABES, SKEEZERS, HOES, TRICKS
Give it a name it's all the same
A bunch of lame ass bitches playin' lame ass games

Shit aint no different, at least not to me
Ladies of the 80's in 2003

Some are little loose, a little bit easy
Some shake their caboose; show a little tit to tease me

Some want to sweat you, cause you're clean at the club
Some wanna ride with you cause you rollin' on dubs
And some need more than 20's they need 23's
yo' shit got to be clean though, plus you blazin' them trees

Shit aint no different, at least not to me
Ladies of the 80's in 2003

You got hood rats with good cats yeah they mixin' it up

You got old ass women makin' them young thangs jealous
You got the preachers wife and daughter doin' a ménage a trois
You got the ladies of Islam, getting' hit, callin' out, Allah

shit aint no different, at least not to me
Ladies of the 80's in 2003

I've seen hookers made housewives and tramps made queens
I've seen lookers turned out right, sellin' they stamps cause they feen
I've seen bad girls clean up and good girls go bad
I've seen retarded girls get sanity while the sane broad went mad
I've seen housewives made hookers and queens made tramps
I've seen stallions go bulimic and medusas turn champs

Shit aint no different, at least not to me
Ladies of the 80's in 2003

I said, shit aint no different, at least not to me
But you can be different; stay focused, and be free

KEEPING IT REAL

Keeping it real is the deal that you feel not to kneel down
Not... saving face as your trading place is a fading taste
And that failing grace is a damn disgrace as you misplace the way you feel now
Do you feel foul because you squeal loud or feel proud of the crows that you've allowed to persuade your most vivid view?
Is it true? Is it you? Or is it that your surrounding is sounding profound yet astounding
as if I heard the words you spoke that joke that didn't even make noise
it didn't even make sense
but sense the pretense of the nonsense
is the fact that you're so dense
acting and reacting like one of those fake boys with those snake ploys and plots
decoys or what nots and those faded glory jeans
and you've traded story scenes
like they're hard boy Levis
your knee highs became
tree highs but we guys despise
true lies
We Just Keepin it Real
        WE JUST KEEPIN IT REAL!!

We mean what we say, we clearly display
We've seen dome dismay
And we feen for the day that seems far away...
Don't run, Brotha stay
I got more shit to say
Fake niggas pull triggas
Real niggas Die quicker
Saggy jeans, Malt liquor,
Can it get any sicker??
Don't get me wrong...
Them 40's pretty nice
And that baggy fit sometimes is the shit I done dared to wear a baggy pair once or twice
Well... the point that I'm making is
You brothas aint takin this fake thang serious and its driving me delirious
But I'm curious about these ludicrous ways you portray your days
And we lie and deceive and you try to believe
The make believe fable...
But aint able
So what's up Brotha ...
My brotha what's the deal

    We Just Keepin It Real
      WE JUST KEEPING IT REAL!!

A LETTER FROM ME FOR ME

I can no longer be concerned about what
you aint learned, you're stubborn, hard
headed and all of the above
You're confusing as hell but I can tell you
don't give a damn about love
It's all about you and what you deem true
From your deepest and darkest dreams
You don't even take time to focus your
mind
And realize shit aint always what it seems
I aint never cheated although I probably
shoulda'
If I woulda' known it could go this route
But I'm better than that even when you
hold back,
cause that aint what I be about
If you was tired of cookin' then damnit
don't do it,
You eat and just feed the kids
I'd figure out what this be about and peep
its some shit I done did
Or rather some shit that I didn't do,
But didn't you say for better or for worse
Then you trip when I speak of how love
makes me weak and how I say you've been
blessed with   a curse
I tell you I miss you, you disregard which
makes it hard, for me to want you back

When we talk on the phone I still feel alone and I'm thinkin' DAMN is it like that
And it really don't have to be that way but you now act so selfishly
Which was really a surprise cause in my eyes that was a way I knew you'd never be
Yet cleverly, you've chosen to run and counseling can't slow you down
Conversations so cold it could've frozen the sun and made some sun flakes fall down
You say I don't care about nobody else only about myself
I say the way you came and stole my soul is just what I call theft
You brought to my attention and thought that you'd mention that you feel I blame our child
But I couldn't blame her cause my problems occurred much later, you know, like now like the day that you told me you was ready to go and you couldn't do this no longer
I figured we'd struggle and fight through the problems and then our love would be stronger
Just when you thinkin' about your future and how you've ridden the drama
I'm face to face with a basket case excuse and you've hidden behind your mama
You've gladly compared me to your daddy, SHIT, I don't drink, I don't smoke, I don't fight

He don't play ball, he don't ski, and this poetry shit, he don't write
You say I'm not strong, independent, or even compassionate
I think I'm fairly strong, pretty independent, and how much compassion can one nigga get
I think you hit it on the head in the letter you wrote; I'd say you said it best
The biggest fact is the way you react to this damn relationship stress
You say it's YOUR issue, but there is no you
You're married, what parts don't make sense
They say it's a thin line between love and hate, well gotdamnit you made it a fence and yeah,
Sometime I procrastinate but I'm movin' at a positive angle
But the quality time with the kids is bullshit, and hell it takes two to tango
I don't ask for relief, cause I take it, and I feel you should take some too
We don't fornicate, we can at least communicate, and when have you taken the kids to the zoo
My mom helps out, but that's alright, she fills in where others can't
The sisters help too, cause that's what they do, except yours, because she just aint
See, I babysat their kids when they needed

It's all in the cipher of life
But don't let the lack of help from your family, make you feel no less of a wife
And I sure aint no less of a man, or a husband even if all of what you said was true
I'd take a bullet to the eye, a knife to the thigh, I've told you I'd die for you
You've said you were stressed, I agree for awhile
Shit, look at all of whose care you've taken
Your mother, father, sister, nephew, brother and I get forsaken
Oh, let's not forget about work, or should I say slavery
You've never took a day or even a lunch to just come and play with me
If I don't work, we don't eat, but you still get a check and heck I got four kids
Cause you best believe, when you up and leave, well not WHEN, cause you already did
That my bills keep glowin' my kids keeps growin' and still there's no escape
I said that when you left was theft
I guess it's more like rape
And through all this since you're new to parenting I hope one thing you've learned is time is exactly like respect, keep workin' and it you will earn

See, time aint free for you or me and LIFE is inconvenient
And so is being in a healthy relationship, so know for real that I've seen it
You're two and out and then you leave your shit just change like the weather
And you had the nerve to say these words, you've been strugglin' with my shit forever
We aint even close, aint even halfway, you just turned quickly departed
You detoured at the fork and made the wrong turn and went right back there where you started
you also mentioned, WE strugglin' together but WE struggled our ass on away
two weeks later, WE got our own place
WE aint got too much to say
But I still miss you ferociously and want you back home right here where you're supposed to be

    This letter aint ever for you to see,
    it's written from me
    FOR ME!

Love IS

Love is not a feeling
It is a situation, without hesitation,
With no explanation, but beyond a man's creation

LOVE IS

Love is chaos and confusion
It is an illusion, a fusion on your mind and soul
Beyond your control to which there's no conclusion

LOVE IS

Love is to forgive the unforgiven
The unlived life that's living
The insane, deranged mentality contained
Yet unconstrained
Within, without, and with whom
It's developed in the room
Enveloped by the womb ... of the universe

LOVE IS

Love is 20/20 vision, correct guesses and respectable decisions
It's a clear view through your rear view
With no blind spot to beware

It's a chance to see what you've been through,
Where you're goin' and why you've got to be there

LOVE IS

Love is like a sin received from the heavens
A blessing from the devil himself
It's the last man standing, the thick and thin friend
When the fair weather fakes have all left
It's the bullet that grazed, the trick that amazed
Left you dazed like an ill with no cure
Love is disease, the cry outs and pleas
The pain in your thigh, the cocaine high
The tribulations and trials you endure

LOVE IS

Love is unreal, even though you can feel
With a grip from the instant you meet
It's the chill of the glass, the frill of the past
It's first place and last, a hint and a dash
Of spice to make the meal complete
It's to live for, to die for, to give for, to cry for,
To write for, to read for, to fight for, to bleed for

It's the want for, the need for, the hunt for, the seed for

LIFE

LOVE IS

BEAUTIFUL

As I peer
    From far or near, the view stays clear
    And you my dear are BEAUTIFUL
BEAUTIFUL as a visionary dessert
    Laced with the sweetest of ingredients
    And covered with a dab of eternal bliss
Baked with the heat of a tender touch
    And browned on the edges, by a gentle kiss
Remember this:
    You are BEAUTIFUL
    BEAUTIFUL at the thought
    Like a dream by a stream with the gleam of the sunrays beaming down,
    Transforming light into a delightful eyeful of unrehearsed perfection
    Adoring the ripples of the behaved waves
    And dipping my feet slightly beneath the water
    To look down and see your reflection
Can I be your protection?
Can I guard your beauty?
    My duty is truly a mission incomplete

And to complete it is my optimum goal and task at hand
I'm asking can,
I be your man … or main squeeze
Suffered through drama from multiple babies mamas and worked around the mental pause,
Caused by the brain freeze
Or lame disease that was passed so fluently
From soul to soul and now you know it's true
Like cooties in a can, I now understand
But enough about me … let's talk about you
You are BEAUTIFUL
BEAUTIFUL to the naked eye, when you're naked I …
See so clearly what flawless by design must entail
and presume like I've been exposed to a bouquet of roses
Unwarned of the thorns that prick me
yet grateful you picked me to view the bloom
Like life, and joy, and greatness …
I hate this when I can't take this
Overabundance of love and put it in proper proportion

   Twisted and knotted, tangled, and confused,
   Mangled and bruised, in a delightful psychological freak show of contortion
     Its extortion
   The way that you're forcing me
   To always be
   A sniper hiding in the brush
     Fighting my crush but feeling the rush …
     of adrenaline that I'm feelin' when you
     come close enough to touch
   you've never heard of such
   Well … I figured that you must not have
     Known or ever been shown the mirror
     at point blank range cause things can change,
     and that duckling that you imagined
     was only a fraction of what you are on the inner
   You're under my skin like a splinter,
   And I need you like a snowman needs winter
   Miss America, You should enter
   Because you are …….BEAUTIFUL

WHO AM I

    I have been
        Oppressed
            Repressed
                Depressed
  And will be pressed ... for time
  Because I'm...

QUESTION
    Who Am I
    Am I the son of a tribal kind?
    Slain by his enemies
    Am I a prophet from the Nile Valley?
    Telling stories of glories that are yet to be seen
    Who Am I
    I am all that can be heard by the spectacular   whispers of the winds
    That travel and unravel times strands
    I'm man's ... child
    Running wild, passing clouds with each step
    As life flurries by
    While some hurry, I
    Back Step
        And
            Reevaluate
                And

                        Focus
on maintaining
                        Huffing
and straining
            No pain then no gaining
        So, the pressure continues
            To push me back
        The pressure continues
            Because I'm black
        The pressure continues
            Because I'm ... that
        Nightfall, darkness, shadow, silhouette
        The universal womb that's still giving birth
        Living in the consequential tomb that we call earth
        But not to die
            And my existence gives life
        My persistence veers strife in another direction
        Look in the mirror and you'll see
            My reflection
        Who Am I
        I am the seed that has been planted in the unfertilized soil of an era
        Where the view is off center and will focus no clearer
        I AM the comb for the nappy head uncivilized boy,

With his pants hanging low and his pistol pointed high

With an empty hollow soul, no love, and no reason why

I AM

HOPE, FAITH, TRUST, Whatever you name it

I AM

the heritage of a nation before plantations,

your history, however you claim it

who am I

you still have no clue

look deep into my eyes and realize

I

AM

YOU

IMAGINARY GAME

      If you love less than I love
          Then why love
          Why try love
          Goodbye love … I'll holla
          Sit back in the 'lac
          Turn up the tracks
              And pop my colla'
          Count my chips and stack my dolla's
          That's how I get down for real
              Hell naw, this aint no joke
          You aint peep the technique of this pimp shit I speak
          I'm the bomb, like that gonja' you smoke
          You know the chronic …
          It's ironic or rather contradicting
          And self-inflicting, not painful though,
          But soothing to your soul
              And your mind
          If you search than you'll find
          And you'll surely be mine
          Just a matter of time
          DAMN BABY YOU FINE
          Naw that aint no line, it's the truth
          You the truth, we the truth and truth is 100 percent fact
          And you know I meant that

    I wouldn't have said it if I didn't
    And if I didn't I wouldn't have said it
    Wouldn't have wrote it if I couldn't
    And if I couldn't you wouldn't have read it
    But it's all in black and white …
    I aint tryin' to mack tonight
      Well maybe a little bit
    But so what, I can't help it if I'm attracted to your mental capacity
    Not to mention my intentions 'cause the thought of that ass-a-be
    I mean … the thought of you has to be strictly from my heart, like love at first sight
    I aint playin', I love you girl, especially if I get it on the first night
    Well, alright …
    You caught me in a lie, but I do,
      Almost, Kinda, Think I like you
      Probably so
    If you give it up easy, you just tryin' to please me
    Baby girl, that don't make you no hoe
    I got more game than the law allow
    So tell me how you like me now
    At least that's what I woulda' said
      If I wasn't so freakin' shy
    But I really ain't SPEAKIN' fly

It's all in my imagination

METAPHORICALLY SPEAKING

    I'm metaphorically speaking while historically seeking
        40 acres without the mule
            I'm no fool,
        I want people, there's no sequel
            You equal the agony
        Please stop draggin' me, BACK
        Cause I'm back again with my men
        And then some, you're holding my knowledge for ransom cause I'm handsome
        Is it the darkness that sparked this?
        Or the attention when you mention the sun tint skin that transcends all opposition
        You hate me, you rape me, you try to escape me, cause you're jealous
        You'd love me if you was me but let's not get overzealous
        It's impossible ... unstoppable is how I'm comin' this century
        Oh ... did I mention wee free now,
            Free how did you come to that conclusion?
        Morpheus explained it to us that, to believe that you're free is dumb
            For freedom is an illusion
        FREE DUMB don't cost a thang
        Check the angle from its obtuse perspective

While the man and the klan combine and expand give me free we demand with no clue or no objective
But ... the true elective is rather subjective and in a hurry will bury his face
While Martin got us startin, to question equals
I guess we get a taste
Or ... at least a little smidgen
Of what the crooks took and a look at what's boilin' in the kitchen
A view at the latter, soon we're shattering our plate
Instead of committin' they keep bullshittin'
You know, they just wanna date
Well, wanna sell us a dream and made it all seem as if freedom is a feasible task
But when questions I ask and get shoved to the last
I'm thinkin' what's stinkin' and realize you said freedom
My ass
Remember I'm
Metaphorically speaking while historically seeking reparations
All my reparations for situations, traumatization's, sterilizations, and the creations of several great nations

        And the creations of several great nations
              I'm ... metaphorically speaking
              While historically seeking, fact
              I'm ... metaphorically speaking
              While historically being black!!!

THE LIFE OF A BROTHA

The life of a brotha
    Is like no other
The trials, tribulations, and struggles don't die
    The life of a black man
        Is hard to understand
        And what's worse is that most folks won't try
            Some people aint concerned
            Some people aint learned
            Some people aint earned the right to call it history
    This knowledge should be called "MY STORY", to most of y'all it's all but a mystery
        We've got nations built on plantations
        We've got situations filled with frustrations
        We've got hatred aimed at the Haitians
        While the lighter folks receive a safe haven
The life of a brotha has long been ignored prostituted and whored
        Our souls been stabbed and jabbed

With the sword of deceit and false intentions
Cheated of our inventions
Retreated in avoidance of lynching's
Worked hard and receive no pensions
Superstitious but true to our religions
      Whatever the faith
      Whatever the case
      Whatever the place
         We're still odd
The life of a brotha is like no other
Because a brother is right next to GOD

ON TOP OF THE WORLD

There's an ant hill that's built on hatred and guilt
    Frustration, anger, and extortion
    Lack of love for self, lack of funds and wealth
    Lack of help or health and opportunities of disproportions
But like contortionists we manage to escape barely damaged
We're the closest to God that you've seen
Though you're not devil by choice
Listen rebels rejoice and hear the voice of a black man who's King
He's explaining to those souls who just didn't know the truth about holding us back
What it means to be last, 400 years past, for my brothers are so blessed to be black
As we focus you notice and we sprout like a lotus, you can't choke us no more, we won't stop
So brothers stand tall, devils will be comin' for ya'll and THIS world,
Now we're right back on top

SHE LOOKED ... I LOOKED

I met her in the mall at Monday night football,
a beautiful young lady with a gorgeous smile and an aura that was glowing like a radiant moon on a cloudlessness night
    And since you know I'm shy, I let her walk by and if it wasn't for her gaze
    I would have regretted for days
    The ways that I allow these strays to leave my sight
She looked... I looked...as if hooked, or addicted, tangled, and constricted,
    Confused and conflicted, entrapped by her stare and
    I'm stuck
    COME HERE< LET ME HOLLA' AT YOU ...
    Incredibly I'm trying my luck
I asked her name, she said, "ROBIN". I thought ...
    I've never met a Robin before
    With her glow still shining and my mind still finding
    New questions in need to know more
I paused for a moment and asked her, her age, she had the most innocent face and childish like quality
    It was a refresher

To meet someone untainted by filth
Till I spiritually took time to undress her
Too good to be true
You know that's what I do, is figure character rather truth or unreal
Her youth would reveal and give me a chance to feel ... her ... out
But, before exchange of numbers, her spiritual brain got dumber and skipped though a range of slop to plop out of her mouth
She asked if I went to church, I said, "NO"
She asked "WHY?" I said I ... Don't do well with organized religion
She said, "PRAY ON IT AND YOU'LL SEE, YOU CAN BE JUST LIKE ME, I RECENTLY FOUND GOD."
And in my brain I heard the psychological collision
SKEEEEEEEEERT, CRASH, BOOM, SMASH
That ass is traveling fast and consequentially she's gently got me bent
You wanna' preach to me, I teach this shit,
Plus she said she got drunk by accident

You're drunk at the mind ... but at the same time, wanna drop lines, of how I can find ... Jesus Christ

Girl you aint nothin' nice, girl you aint nothin' nice

Yeah, I had to say it twice
That wasn't the end though of our talk
Now it's my turn so you listen and learn
cause I'm that nigga that walks the walk

I'm not religious at all

But I still stand tall

While you fall ... flat on your neck

I don't smoke, drink, eat pork, litter and I'm sure it's some other shit, let me check

Never cheated on my wife,
    (When I was married)

Am respectful as hell, hell I've never even called a woman a whore
    (To her face)

And can take a situation put it down in dictation for all women,

I always open doors
    (My momma taught me that)

But on the other hand, obviously don't understand ... religion

So keep readin' that book, keep feedin' that crook

While he's rollin' that two thousand and ten

And don't trip on the day when judgment takes place and J.C. comes to punch you in the chin,
    and you didn't get in
        Oh yeah, she wasn't feelin' my kids
           she definitely made that clear
But I aint lost no love cause her lack thereof, aint shit, and I'm dad of the year
    She said she was lookin' for the one
...
    I guess kinda' like Neo from the Matrix
    But see, I've been the one, two, and three,
    Got girls chain' me, but at the end of the day, I damn near hate chics
    Can't live with 'em
    Can't live with 'em
    You aint know, the crazy, here's the bus, ALL ABOARDS
And ROBIN, good luck, hope you find your Neo
But please sober up before you lookin' for the LORD

MY THOUGHTS

My thoughts
      Are just that
Dreams and ideas that seem all too clear
But the trail sometimes is a drab one
I reach and stretch with intent to fetch
A flawless catch of my visions with decisions
To grab one, jab one
LEFT, RIGHT, LEFT
A knockout with immense precision
My decision of no religion has no bearing
On what's righteous, I might just
NOT have the time
NOT know the time
NOT care of the time being that time is of
the essence
My being is of the presence
Of
My thoughts
My thoughts
      Are just that

Fantasy, Reality
Formality, Technicality, no belief but I
Believe I will receive through spirituality
There is no finality, no finish, and no end
Transcending begins the tide that bring in
And washes away the harshness of day
But the night brings out the starts
The darkness shines brightly

I might be politely reciting my writing or fighting just slightly
To become one from Venus not Mars
To overstand a woman's point of view
To point at you
And say softly
These are my thoughts
My thoughts
    Are just that
A view manifested
A few men arrested
For the fight of the masses and we wuppin white asses
    For a change
No really,
    FOR a change of the woes
As deranged as our foes
We've aimed for the pros
But we've strangled our souls
Niggas now, not Negroes
But we'll be back to endeavor
And be blacker than ever
Once we take time to sever
The head from the snake
And I dread to be fake
We's Americans turned African
Laugh again
I know we will
COLORED BOY, JIGGABOO, SPADE, NIGGA, COON

KING, SOLDIER, SCIENTIST, WOMB OF CREATION,
WHITE MAN'S GOD and that tickles me still
That's what they thinkin
But that's how we feel
Beware if I scare or frighten I'm just writin',
No offense if I enlighten
These are just
My Thoughts
My thoughts
      Are just that

LOVE YOURSELF

What's up foxy lady?
Im tryin' to give you all of what you need

Tryin' to stress you the fuck out,
Eliminate your will to succeed

I'm tryin' to make you feel some things

You aint never felt before

To show you how much I truly care,
I'll use an extension cord

And when I get drunk and come back home,
My dinner better be cooked

You remember last time I showed you my love,
The next day the way that you looked

Those two black eyes and fractured nose
And your jaw just wired shut

And don't forget my affectionate words:
I hate you, you bitch, you slut

I caress you with tender accusations;
Like I know you're sleepin' around

What took you so long to get home from work?
Even though you gig across town

The more I show my love,
The harder I tend to shove 'em

I curse you, beat you, and eat your soul
You stay, "because I love 'em"

And if you're stayin' and takin' my love
Regardless of your health

Don't surrender cause you love me
Leave cause you love yourself

DRAMA

Drama surrounds me and encloses swiftly
As if to capture my spirit
And entrap it within the dungeon of no escape,
But, what have I done?

I've been blessed with a family of my own, and to share that
Is an option that seems far too real
And far too harsh for a man that's seeking tranquility, and civility, and unselfishness.

But again, this is the real world.
Live, is truth
The universe slowly seems to unravel as if a mummified entity is having bandages removed, one after another only to discover that emotion and devotion are unobtainable
By those that have no peace within

Where am I? Why am I shackled and surrounded? Why have I been hackled and hounded?
Plummeted and pounded, and astounded by the serpent
Who convinced me to eat of the forbidden tree?

And why am I to be punished, tainted, and blemished
Only to be informed I'm finished,
My cipher has been broken and the Bible has spoken of me

Yet, now I see and stand strong,
Now I feel the rights and wrong,
Now I am as a god, to know all and to be one with infinity
      I AM MAN
      I HAVE CHILD
And with woman we complete the whole trinity

Patience seems to relieve itself of my grasp, escaping the confinements of my eternal captivity
Running free thought the jungle and swinging from vine to tree
And wheezing for one last breath as he plunges himself into the upward flowing waters of the Nile
While, I still remain in disdain and insecurity,
Being watched over by the corrupted knights
Who silently guard the walls of my unescapable shell

This unescapable hell is what I know

And it travels from my soul, to soul, to soul, to soul,
In a feverish attempt to tempt the hearts of men
And to implode as it erodes my spine
To leave as a hollow stump of a man
I once wished that life would get better,
But I realized that this shell that has me trapped
Is ultimately protection against the cancerous filled poisons
That tries to contaminate my inner sanctum

So, as I have been sentenced to life…within and without,
I must say quietly in your ear, come closer
… No More Drama!!!

LISTEN CLOSELY OR JUST BE DUMB

Listen closely, cause there's a lesson to be learned
Beds to be burned, heads will be turned,
But that's not my concern
See, just when you thought it could get no worse,
There's and encore performance with the extended verse
THE RE-MIX
See, these chics just take advantage when there's an advantage to be take
The bible says forsake all others, bow the hell's I get forsaken
You fryin' up shit 'fore I even bring home the bacon,
And then get mad when I ask what you makin'
I never thought I'd say this but ...
BITCHES AINT SHIT BUT HOES AND TRICKS
And now that I think about it, that shit makes sense
If the shoe fits wear it, if it don't then let it go
Only problem is every once in a while, we do love these hoes
And I don't mean hoes like you fuckin' and suckin'

And getting' slapped by a nigga wit' a perm
I use that word to give an idea and for lack of a better term
I give a mother fucka' a foot they want two feet, an arm, and a leg
I give your ass an omelet, a whole damn chicken
You get pissed; say you just wanted an egg
I can't win for loosin', can't heal for bruisin'
And can't move forward for back peddlin'
I've always said you never know till it's over
The true nature of the beast remained hidden
And the more that's revealed, the more that I feel it's a joke and you got to be kiddin'
But puttin' all your jokes aside, regurgitation' my swallowed pride,
I've realized you weren't ready for the man I've become
And you fronted like you were; now our history's just a blur
And I guess to expect any different would
        Just be Dumb!

I HATE LOVE

They say that hatred is unhealthy
    That means that I'll probably die young
I've been drained by love and strained by love
    And resent the things that she's done
She taunts me, She haunts me, She teases me
    As she runs in the other direction
She gracefully re-enters my realm as I quickly take cover
    And seek protection
As I gaze in the mirror her reflection ...
    I see like ghost from the past at last I ask... why me?
But no answer seems clear and hearts filled with fear
And I hear a soft voice in my head
    Oh, it's that voice in my ear that won't disappear that keeps getting louder instead
This love chic is hectic, she's yearning for blood
And she won't stop until she's milked you dry
    I hate love with a passion and I guess that I'll tell you why

She's a selfish, "B" I'm sorry, I'll try to refrain from profanity
She's mentally manipulative and lives life on the borderline of insanity
She comes as she pleases and stays as she will
    She says what she wants to and goes where she feels
She's kinda like a beast uncaged, wild and on the prowl
At night if you listen close enough, sometimes you can hear her howl
And her victims are usually randomly picked; you never know who's next
    Preventative maintenance is a one night stand
    Cause quite often she'll attach during sex
She also harnesses a certain power that causes mind control
    I hate love, boy I hate love, but I hate to see her go
She makes you do stuff that you've never done
And things that you'd never do
    She even makes you write about her
    No, really it's true
I hate love, boy I hate love, but I hate to see her go
    SHHH … I think she's leaving now, she's just movin' pretty slow

HOUSEWIFE INTO A HOE

The say never turn a hoe into a housewife
    But, why not is the question that I ponder
So let's hike blindly into the wilderness of marital corruption
    And see how far off we can wander
I DON'T DO THAT!
DO YOU THINK I'M SOME TYPE OF WHORE?
    But a hoe will say I've never been treated this way
    I'm going to do this though I've never done it before

    A housewife stops fucking pretty quick and head is even less than none
    But a hoe is good to go five days in a row
    Plus she likes giving head for fun

    A housewife suspects that you're cheating when you come in at 3 A.M.
    But a hoe comes in talks about her date with some nigga,
    And tells you how she played him
    Then she hands you some bread and gets ready for bed
    Cause its 3:30 A.M. and time is overdue

But when you're ready to snooze
You must have her confused
Cause the hoe is in the buff straddling you

Now don't get me wrong, I love my wife and wouldn't trader her for a million bucks
But sex with a hoe is as good as it gets
And sex with a housewife sucks … if you're lucky

GOOD GUYS

           Here I go again
                 As always, good guys finish last
                 In the hundred yard dash of life
                 I could drown in a splash
                 Emblaze by an ash
                 Get married and still not have a wife
                       ONLY ME …
        I'm really just ventin'
                 Cause again I've been bitten by the lion that some call a kitten
                 The brothers that cheat and lie
                 Are the ones that seem to fly
                 And get by through a life of bullshittin'
                       BUT NOT ME …
        I think I should cheat 'em and beat 'em
                 Fuck 'em and feed 'em soup
                 Or just scream 'em and don't feed 'em at all
                 Rather you do 'em right or wrong,
                 Your game is lame or strong
                 You get gonged or they're blockin' out your call

Either way when you're true
    And you do what you do
    And they're doin' it to
    And it seems that all is a blast
Look for the knife in your spine
    Cause my wife gave me mine
I still find that GOOD GUYS finish last

AM I LOCKED IN?

RDC ...
That's where I be
A convict ...
Yeah, I guess that's me
They take my blood here and test my health
No longer is my life lived in stealth
There're no more lies and no more deceit
I played the game, face it, I just got beat
But at least now I eat three meals a day
And I take time to read and take time to pray
See, it aint all the bad, you know, with time comes change
And with this change also came brains
It's kind of weird, you know this whole situation
Writing folks, telling jokes, exercise, and getting wise
    That's incarceration
I'm not here to complain but to explain this place
Not to warn you but inform you, see these experiences I can't replace

Sometimes I wonder, sometimes I think about …
If I am really locked in or if maybe you're locked out.

I've been here 19 days in a place I can't even leave
But the things that happened on the outside is what I find hard to believe
A cousin died from a gunshot wound
And right at this moment a homey lies in a hospital room
They say he's got to lose a leg, DAMN, now that's sad
So I can't really complain, it really aint all that bad
I mean … I'm still alive, my health is great
It could be worse aint no tellin' with fate
It's kind of safe in here though,
    I know you probably doubt
But I wonder if I'm locked in or if maybe you're locked out.

UNTITLED

Rainbows collide and combine joining into a
visual kaleidoscope of dreams and hopes
With prayers and layers
Of an ethnic balance unmatched by most
Communities of the uncivilized
While masses have united
Classes have decided, to take marinated
and documented, deceptive discriminated
pieces
      and re-write it
Oh say, can you see, blindly
I visualize the disguise of the beast
As the MATRIX unravels and the black man
travels through time
See I'm what some call a nigga, who'd
figure
Usually it's while my backside is facin' their
mouth
While some don't barr cause they reside so
far ...
Deep, Deep, DEEP down in the South
But up North it's with a snicker
Cause in an instant or quicker
It's a million of us plus seven
With Lil' Man Man, N'EM, and Ray Ray
And Big Momma, and some white folks
Who too, wanna reach heaven
So next time you say nigga
See whose team is bigger

And peep how we all can unite
Cause we die for dumb shit, EVERYDAY, that I love
SO we sho' aint scared to die for what's right

ADDICTED

It doesn't take long since my addiction is strong
The withdrawal takes an immediate toll
I fight off the urge and still I splurge
No control … I'm losing my soul
At night my sleeps interrupted by dreams
That seems to've gone bad
Insanity concludes my confused translucent illusions
My thoughts would appear I've gone mad
CRAZY
For the vibe I receive I can't believe my mind
Rambles in an untraditional state
If you've never seen what it means to fiend
Then I'm positive you can't relate
But if you've ever desired in your body and brain
Then multiply the pain by eight
That's the torture I've been introduced to
Since I'm used to
Spending every day with my mate

I'm addicted

I'M BALLIN'

I SLANG HOPE LIKE DOPE, SPEND EVERY
NIGHT ON THE BLOCK
STEADY PUSHIN' THIS PRODUCT
AND MY WRITINGS THE ROCK
MOVIN' WORDS LIKE BIRDS DROPPIN'
NOTHING' BUT WEIGHT
COOKIN' UP 19 BRINGING BACK 28
I USUALLY COP A HUNDRED WHOLE ONES
SOMETIMES I MAKE IT FROM SCRATCH
THAT'S WHY THEY CALL ME KINGPIN NOW
I SELL A TOP QUALITY BATCH
AND FOR THAT JOKER WHO WANTS
MEDIOCRE
GO SEE THEM FOOLS DOWN THE STREET
'CAUSE I KEEPS MY STUFF "P"
IF YOU DON'T COP, YOU DON'T EAT
AND IF YOU DON'T WANT WHAT I'M
SELLIN',
I'LL GIVE YOU A SAMPLE, NOW YOU'RE
TWEAKED
STANDIN' IN LINE WHILE I GRIND
HOPIN' TO GET A DOUBLE UP EVERY TIME
THAT WE SPEAK
AND IF YOU NEED 2 FOR 15, I'LL GIVE YOU 1
AND A HALF
BREAKIN' MY WHOLE ONES DOWN
TO SYLLABLES, HOMEY, YOU DO THE MATH
EVEN WHEN YOU CITY IT, MY WORKS STILL
NUMBING YOUR BRAIN

INSPIRED BY MY REALITIES, RATHER PLEASURE OR PAIN
YOU THINK YOU HAD SOME GOOD, INJECT MY SMACK IN YOUR SOUL
I'M DOIN' BIG THANGS, BALLIN' OUT OF CONTROL
I GOT STARTED HITTIN' AND MISSIN' JUST DOIN' ENOUGH TO GET BY
EVEN DROPPIN' IT IN SCHOOL ZONES, GET THE WHOLE COMMUNITY HIGH
IF I CAN GET YOU WHILE YOU'RE YOUNG THEN, I KNOW I GOT YOU WHEN YOU'RE OLD
THE SOONER I GET YOU SPRUNG, THE MORE WORK TO BE SOLD
AND IF YOU NEED ME TO FRONT YOU SOME,
JUST MAKE SURE YOU HANDLE YOUR BIZ
BREAK ME OFF SOME ON THE BACK END, WITH KNOWLEDGE BLAZIN' LIKE GIZ
THE POLICE RAIDED MY SPOT, I GOT IT HOT AND ON STINK
GARBAGE BAGS FULL OF INFORMATION LIKE I WAS THE COLUMBIAN LINK
I'M TRYIN' TO LOCK THE WHOLE WORLD DOWN
ESPECIALLY SISTERS AND BRO'S
I'M DOIN' BIG THANGS, BALLIN' OUT OF CONTROL
I SLANG HOPE LIKE DOPE, INJECT MY SMACK IN YOUR SOUL

GET YOU ADDICTED TO THIS KNOWLEDGE,
IM BALLIN' OUT OF CONTROL

WHEN I RETURN

I never knew how much I cared
    When in my view at you I stared
The moments together that which we shared
    Till I turned and you were no longer there
For a while I had to say
    But pride kept leaping in my way
I miss you, really indeed I do
    The pain inside my dear has grew
Feeling you near me dwells in my brain
    I miss you dearly but I fight the pain
For only your touch can ease the burn
    I hope you're there when I return

I never knew the prize I had,
    A priceless gem for sure
This love disease of lonesomeness,
    Of which you are the cure
You'd never know I felt this way,
    I'd never know myself
Except now that we are apart,
    I feel like someone else
See, you were a part of me unknown to many through the naked eye
But deep within, on through my skin
    Without you the old me would die
Although it's not your fault I'm here,
    Your heart must control

To call me near when I leave here
        So I can again be whole
So of this love I'm teaching you,
        It's up to you to learn
A reminisce of our first kiss,
        Please be there when I return

TRAPPED

Trapped my brother ... indeed, indeed
    No more shall my wants exceeds my needs
Trapped my brother so please take heed
    See ... just like me, you also bleed

You claim your blood contains so much rage
    But still ... you're trapped inside this cage
You claim your blood pumps steel ...
    Well I guess
Cause that would surely make you the best

Do you mind my friend if I quiz you though?
    If you're so great ... then why not go
I mean ... this cage couldn't hold you if steel you bleed
    But you're still trapped my brother
    Indeed, Indeed

TOO GOOD

        They say if it's too good to be true
            Then it is exactly that indeed
        But, if it doesn't feel too good
            Then how good could it possibly be
        Some things are nice, precisely
            But nice is only fair
        Good, is a wee bit better than that?
            Yet still only half way there
        Great, is a force to be reckoned with?
            Give credit when credit is due
        But nothing seems to be good enough
            Unless it is too good to be true

YOU ARE

You are my earth, my air, my fire and my water
My mate, my wife, my soul, my life
The essence of our daughter
To live without you, is not to be alive
But ... to just be
And love is all that I know of you
And you have made truth of me
      You are all that is good ... like a goddess in an Egyptian land
When I wandered the world and was misunderstood
It was you who could truly understand
      You are reason, and reality, format and technicality
The vision of a blind man's perception
Even before your birth, a world was your worth, and your existence
IMMACULATE CONCEPTION

You are the starts that shine like a spotlight on my path ...
      and illuminate any that should be seen
If heaven is a kingdom, cause that's what I hear,
Then, of that, you must be queen
Your presence is like presents to a child deprived ...
      And has never received such a gift

Your voice is a hymn, I desire your choir
And your solo will help to uplift

You Are All, You Are Everything, You Are a universe in a whole
You Are Friend, You are Family, You Are Spirit, You Are Soul

You Are

AUTOBIOGRAPHY

The circumstances seem to be strange
      Even though you have no clue
I will take this time to express my thoughts
      And explain myself to you
Although we've never sat to chat
      With this description I'll begin
I'm tall with love and fat with understanding
      With wisdom colored skin
My hair is long with pleasantness
      The roots show a shade of passion
I dress in sensitivity to keep up with the latest fashion
My eyes are colored with emotion
      When I'm high on life they form a haze
I work at ROMANCE VALUE MART, nights
      And Knowledge Mall on days
On Saturday and Sunday
      I'm part-time help at CARE-A-LOT
I live on the corner of Lonely Lane
      But Moral Avenue is my hang out spot
Oh, I forgot to tell you my first name is Loving
      Togetherness is my last
In the future I see respect
      So disregard my past
      SO ... YOU LOVE MUSIC?

Could I be music to your ear?
When I'm near you hear the acoustics but fear that the song will last a short time

Could I be a number announced from the tips of your lips?
An audio logical miracle, a lyrical spiritual, a tuned by nature
And by character combined we rhyme

I'm the rat tat that's played, as the world sways to the rhythmic melodic vibes
I'm the words that's heard over laid back tracks
The drum beat created and demonstrated and the chants of the African tribes

Could I be that ballad, so valid you auscultation absorbs and consumes
NOT HISTORY, yet historical
Never to forget the sublime mind advances as I enter your auditorical womb

I'm the mysterious minstrel, overheard by mistake as you take a ride down the hi fi road
I'm the mass capacity CD changer, THE A.M. and F.M. mode

I'm every song your heart desires, retire the singles you must rewind
Could I be the music that you love so much?
Cause I'm sure that you could be mine
So ... you love music?

GOOD NIGHT

Humility evolves
Tranquility dissolves
Stability resolves

All confusion, lack of focus
To view the true face of the case of the hocus pocus

Can I get a witness?
To insist the illness and for realness
Of the plague and curse
As the beggin' hurts
And the pressures worse, or more so
Quick to click when you see a chic
Walk by my mind's eye with a wiggle
That jiggles a little as I peep the swivel of her torso

It's just a glance of the walkin' dance of the anus
Nothin' major still painless, you thought I was brainless?
Not that much and not enough to touch
The butt and clutch a freaky deaky kinky slut
Cause I love you and it feels right
Even when your hugs are like drugs
When the pharmacies closed

Like coke with a sneeze never to reach my nose ... ALL OVER THE FLO'
Looking for smidgen
Getting played like the NBA on a team full of midgets

SHE LOVES ME

She loves me not
SHE LOVES ME, I hope, cause I just couldn't cope
Have to find me a rope, and, yeah right,
Find me a rope so I can tie up my boat
Even though it don't float
I'm a set sail some night
WITH YA
Without ya
WITH YA, cause it's a life long journey
I agreed to set sail

I'll be damned if I surrender, I'm no pretender
I don't fail
It's all real ... like a dead body
Layin' naked in the alley
I'm here for you, takin' it like Malcom X at a Klan rally

The things I do for you
I guess for me, cause I truly see
It takes we to be happy

FUCK IT, I love you, GOOD NIGHT

DOUBLE PARKED

I accidentally left my heart
    Double parked ...
    At 71st and Michigan Road
Next thing I know, when I come back to go
    I realize my shit's been towed
So I ... go downtown and pay my fees
    Boy, they be stickin'
    But you gotta' pay
I'm thinkin' it's cool; I'll just drop this cheese ...
    And then I'll be on my way
But the officer said, "HOLD UP BROTHA',"
    "I need to holla' at you for a minute!"
So now I'm gettin' anxious cause you know 5-0 is dangerous
    And I politely say, "yes sir, what is it?"
The popo says, "YOU GOT WARRANTS AND STUFF, SO DON'T MAKE US GET ROUGH."
He peeps the bling of my wedding ring
    He said, 'DAMN NIGGA, YOU TRYIN' TO BLIND ME, YOU KNOW THAT'S ASSAULT!"
    And I suffered a RODNEY KING
Now my eyes is black, my ass is blue
    And my lips a little bit red
But I can't even trip; I'm excited and shit,

        Cause I damn near thought I would be dead
So I go get my heart, had to catch a cab ...
        50 dollars
        DAMN! I almost clicked
I did have a ride but they cut out, when I was sittin' there gettin' my ass kicked
Now you all know the stories, about INDY TOW
        And the problems you're bound to face
So I look for my heart, it's almost torn apart,
        Plus, someone stole my I.V. case
My ticker's missin' from my trunk,
        There goes my thump and the wires is ripped off my amp
        And I need a jump ...
        CLEAR
Now it's time for me to break camp
So on my way home, I ride tre' eight
Look at my watch and see that it's late,
So I hurry to be on my way
Get to my crib and my wifey is gone
        HELL NAW!
What an F'd up day
She said I was out in the streets doin' some wrong,
She swear that a nigga is foul
Only thing I could do is laugh to myself
And out loud I shouted out
        WOW!

Well the moral to this tale, is all can be well,
And like lightening the bullshit can start
So think about what you do and think about what you don't
And most of all, be careful where you park your heart

CONTINUE TO SPROUT

My seeds continue to sprout
The children pout as Daddy shouts
Because they've all welcomed the wear out
    But this is still home
This is where they live at; this is where I forgive at
Sometimes you'll hear, WHO DID THAT
Or
MAN, SO FAST YOU'VE GROWN
I've given life to an array of me-ites, mini me's
Or simply put, the kids
My future is set in stone
My history will be far from a mystery and my struggles will set the tone
See … kids look at the path that I've taken,
Shaking branches as I rigorously hiked through times' jungle-like arena
Dodging the lions, and tigers, and bears, oh my!
As I stay poised just like a ballerina
But … sometimes my dance is not so perfect
Not graceful, still though, I try my best
They teach me the steps they've choreographed
And tutor me for life's biggest test
I'm the pupil, now I see
I'm not teaching the child how to live …
My children are teaching me

SO FAST YOU'VE GROWN DAD, YOU'VE ALMOST GOT IT
KEEP TRYIN' SCOOTER YOU'LL GET IT
And as my seeds sprout into trees you'll hear me shout
"I DID IT!"
Excited and enlightened, still frightened by the unpredictable storms that lie so far in front
Trying to provide what you need and to understand what you want
You're special to me; my void is filled by an overabundance of bliss that you bring along
Your growth is a ballad of beautiful to my ears
And I'm enthused just as I sing along
And I'm enthused just as I sing along
In the background I watch curiously lurking from the bushes
Careful not to extend many shoves for love sometimes causes pushes
My children are my fix, my habit, my dope
My seedlings are my magic, my reason and
      My Hope!!!

BLACK WOMAN

BLACK WOMAN
    You are my Nubian queen
    The ruler in my life
BLACK WOMAN
    You are the goddess of hue
    To only be a god's wife
BLACK WOMAN
    You are the female sovereign
    To govern over my domain
BLACK WOMAN
    My lady of divine femininity
    Only you can break these chains
BLACK WOMAN
    You are the monarch of colored beauty
    Outside and deep within
BLACK WOMAN
    You are my pigmented princess
    Your kingdom I shall defend
BLACK WOMAN
    You are my supreme brown skinned diva
    You're the best there will ever be
BLACK WOMAN
    You are my chocolate Aphrodite
BLACK WOMAN ... you made me ... Me

BLACK MUSIC

What is it we do that stimulates, you emulate and duplicate

Black Music

You pick and choose and abuse but still loose,
    Left dazed and amazed and confused,
    Because it's something you can't do

You can't relate, translate, or create
    You just remake, what we make
    And swear that you can't be fake
    But we know the truth

Black Music
    Is the alpha and the omega
    The genesis without the sega
    It's like a playstation for CD's
    With MC's, R and B's celebrities
    Filled with Lauryns, Marys, Ice Cubes and Ice T's
You fill me?

Black Music
    We use it, we lose it
    We find it, rewind it
    And play again

Fast forward the distorted
Black Music is the SHIT
Excuse me, let me say again
Black Music is the SHIZNIT
It's the bomb diggity like WHOA!
It makes you sing My, My, My
While playing basketball with Kurtis Blow
It makes you walk this way
And go call Tyrone
No scrubs allowed on this scene
So share my world since it aint my fault
That Black Music continues
To Bling Bling

THINK OF ME

Think of me when you are alone and you
don't understand why it is, you only
Think of me when being alone or with a
group you still feel lonely

THINK OF ME

Think of me when the guy you're with
makes you open up your own door
Think of me when being a friend to your
mate seems like a chore

THINK OF ME

Think of me when there are no jones, no
fun, no new experiences
Think of me where there's no one to talk to
and there hasn't been ever since

THINK OF ME

Think of me when you need a shopping
buddy but no one wants to go
Think of me when your spirit gets hungry
because I'm food for your soul

THINK OF ME

Think of me when the sun comes up and the view is not the same
Think of me when you want to play but you cannot find the game

THINK OF ME

Think of me when your back is sore because, in forever it hasn't been rubbed
Think of me when you want to party, but feel out of place at the club

THINK OF ME

Think of me when the T.V.'s on and the picture just doesn't come on clear
Think of me when your skies seem cloudy and you need a new atmosphere

THINK OF ME

Think of me when your child needs extra love and tender care
Think of me when you can barely breathe because there's no love in the air

THINK OF ME

Think of me when the man of your house decides that he's not coming home

Think of me when reality hits and you're exhausted of being alone
THINK OF ME

THE REASON I'M A GOD

No colored allowed BOY ...

To the back of the bus NIGGA ...
    Or
We don't serve your kind
These are phrases society seems to bring to mind
    Or
When you say I'm not prejudice but ...
That but, makes you an ass
I see right through that head of yours
As if your skull was glass
And when you call me boy
I guess you just don't understand
I was born a male, so you can tell Massa;
I'm a young man
A black man born the underdog
But bred to be a KING
A thorn in the devil's hoof
An arrow in his wing
A chip in the horns upon his head
A snag of his tail so odd
Because I'm black, exactly that
Is the reason that I'm a god

KNOW WHAT I MEAN

I still await your touch black woman
    Queen of the realm which I dwell
But it seems as though my soul is transparent
    And you know me a bit too well
When I called, you came, when I came you called
    What a combination we were like a dream
But situations have changed and relations estranged
    A V-8 couldn't straighten love's lean
This journey of ours, a safari in the woods
    There's no focus our compass is broke
I ask how you feel, you shun to reveal
    And your emotions are buried in smoke
The foundation which we stood seemed sturdy
And strong I guess I was wrong and fell through
And strong I guess I was wrong and fell through
    I dangle by thread; I'm starving unfed and can only be nourished by you
The officials say foul so I give it a shot
    But the line doesn't appear to be free

Every time I get close to you, you still pull away
        From the arc so you're spacing by three
I'm hot like hell in June, July, and horny like Satan's head
        But you're cold like Alaska at Christmas time
Layin' flat on an ice skating bed
You lovin's like bowling 12 strikes in a row
        It's perfect and lucky to be seen
I hope that this helps to show its felt
        When I want you, you know what I mean

FOREVER TOUCHED

I feel as though you're raping my soul
    Please be gentle as caressing begins
Take your time undressing my mind
    And pleasure shall surely transcend
KNOWING that you are my first should
explain the nervousness
KNOWING that my thirst is not perverse
    It's just that I've never done this
before
I've never felt this stiffness below
My jisms strong
I've never been touched or have touched so
deeply
It feels good but I hear that it's wrong
Some say a virgin is scared
I SAY, take it!!!
For real this time I'm all yours
No locks, No Chains, No Work, NO Chores
Be gentle, Be soft, Be sure, Be pure
Be sacred and sincere
Cause the doors are all wide open
As I'm coping with this desire to be
Moonlight kiss played live by the Sea
And Wind tunes
As the breeze is a tease and it's cool
Since
NO means NO
So I go lay nude in the dunes
Building me a castle of the sands

I'm no less of a man
Just because your touch is first
It's where you fondled my beating rhythm
And how you eager my thirst
Someday real soon or
Later I guess
I'll suggest that you view back on this first time endeavor
I gave you all of me
    See sex aint shit
    It's my heart and soul
    That you've touched
    And
    Touched it forever

A BRIGHER DAY

I will not be broken and used
    Battered and bruised
Confused by your haunted ways
    No more will your darkness
Overcome my light to dim the brightness of my days

STAND BACK

I have been a slave,
    A pawn, a prisoner, and still
I stand as a man
    A hero amongst common folks
A giant along the land
    You cannot and will not drain my spirit, my body, or my mind
As you attempt to hide my glory
    I rummage through life to find the energy to scorn your wicked woes
    Our kindred spirits estranged
Your dysfunctional and disproportional ideas
Clearly need help to change
    Life is simple, but living's a task
    And don't ask for help show pride
    A prideful fool obeys wrong rules, and dies of spiritual suicide
But I live on with heart in hand and love is locked away

I'll never let you dim my light
        Tomorrow's a brighter day

A DRIVE IN THE DARK

A drive in the dark
A swim with the sharks
      All a walk in the park compared to
my life
Barefoot on hot coals
A devil hunting for souls
      Still my only fear is at night with my
wife
Not really of her
It's still a bit blurred
      I see myself out in the streets
searching for fresh flesh
But I calm myself swift
Cause a wife is a gift
      And her actions must all be a test
Is it Devil or God?
Osiris or Nimrod
      I'd hate to think it could be worse
At least it's clear as day
What I mean when I say
      That true love means you're blessed
with a curse!

MY THEORY OF RELATIVITY

That which makes you laugh
    May also make me cry
That which makes you live
    Could be the same which makes me die
And that thing that causes your death
    Could somehow save my life
And that broad that you call Bitch
    Might someday be my wife

It's All Relative Baby, it's All Relative

That piercing in your nose
    Looks to me just like a hole
My energy causes my aura
    You know that thing that you call a soul
You worship Yahweh, Jesus, Jehovah, Mary, and Allah
    I pay homage to Horus, Heru, Osiris, Isis, and Amen Ra
This theory of relativity
    To me is just common sense
There's my side and there's your side
    Two sides to every fence

It's All Relative Baby, It's All Relative

WHAT IS LOVE

What is love?
Do we know by chance?
Could be emotion
Could be circumstance

They say it's a feeling, a very intense concern
But the more that I experience this,
The less that it seems that we'll learn
The harder we strive, the harder the task
More often than not,
I plot just to ask
Is Love a true edifice
A structure built tall,
Or a temporary standby thought that's on call
If it's real then it's permanent,
Eternity and plus
Ashes to dust infinity of us

What is Love?
Do we know by chance?
Could be emotion
Could be circumstance

LOVE'S RESSURECTION

Dreary eyes peer down from a cloudy sky
    Upon the heart of an empty soul
The tears of a man are so intense to
withstand this pain, one should woe
As days pass slowly and nightfall seems to
allow
    Dreams to find peace in my mind
The mental storms damage thoughts of
tranquility
    Leaving stability dangling behind
I'm awaiting the bliss of midnight kiss
    And I'm forsaken
Though the illusions conclude something
real
    The truth is final
Misty visions arrive swiftly just to breathe
    I believe it could kill;
But my spirit manifests
My lungs expand with each whiff of your
velvety flesh
Your cinnamon scented poison is like candy
to taste
    And your love is a duel to the death
    Willing I am, to die if I must
With a lust for a love of such perfection
Able to strengthen the weak, make the
tongue less speak
    While my dying ways blaze
    Your resurrection

LISTEN

Listen to the secrets that I unleash
Listen to the mysteries that rest in peace
Listen to the whispers of cloudless sky
Listen and don't ask why

No Questions

JUST KIDDIN

When I met her she was smokin'
    Tryin' to crack by provokin'
conversation
    Cause my demeanor was piss
Came over to my table
    Tryin' to be in my stable
    But not able, yet sincere to insist
So I asked her, her number
    Couldn't have got any dumber
I fell for the okey doke
I shoulda known she was alone
    For a reason not shown
Plus she was smellin' like mary jane smoke
    Eyes blood shot red life a fiend in
the dark
    Tryin' to spark up
Conversation from a baller
Had to ask her, her age
    Cause I couldn't engage
In conversation but I agreed to call her
When I called her we did breakfast
    At a rinky dink spot
Making sure that no one would see me
Finally, hooked up again
    I was hittin' the skins
Next thing I know her ass couldn't leave me
Now I'm trapped in this life
    With kids and a wife

All because of the way I was hittin'
I don't even like her
      At times wanna' strike her
Of course you know I'm just kiddin'

I SENSE WITHIN

Within your eyes I witness pain
    You are mesmerized with fear
Within your lips I hear the frustration
    Of speaking to me from here
Within your ears you internalize
    A millennium of conscious ways
Within your fingertips you hold
    My heart for infinite days

Within your eyes I see the light
    That glows upon my face
Within your lips I absorb your drips
    It is passion that I taste
Within your ears I enchant your mind
    With bliss to your mentality
Within your fingertips you've grasped my dreams
    And created a reality

Within your eyes I can view right through
    To the bareness of your soul
Within your lips to kiss I'd swoon
    For achieving my optimum goal
Within your ears my voice will announce
    My love time and time again
Within your fingertips you feel my heart
    And that which I sense within

HAPPY ANNIVERSARY

How long has it been?

A month or two?

Not more it's been too good

You've made me feel a love so real

Though I thought I never could

I now understand how sacrifice

Creates pleasure in the end

And soon you'll be my beloved wife

And still remain my friend

Happy Anniversary

GLAD THAT THEY KNEW US

Can I borrow your brain?
        As your sorrow enflames
So tomorrow the rains may uncover
        The truth in your past
        Your youth in a flash
As we splash in the puddle of lovers
It's a must that we hold
        And a plus twenty fold
For this story that's told for far too often
        A heart that is scarred
        Is a heart that is hard?
Don't disregard cause a charred heart may still soften
So take heed as I speak
        For my knees getting weak
        Through the trees I must seek my salvation
As I trek through the woods
        I expect that the goods
Which were sought can be caught by love's relations
When it's over and done
        We will shine like a sun
That will stun the whole world as they view us

They will see that it's me
        And it's you and our seeds
And indeed all folks glad that they knew us

DEATH

Death engulfs the lives I see
I Run I Hide I Cry I Flee
I Plea I Beg Don't take me yet
But why the fear
      Is death a threat?

To answer that no human can
It's never been reached by Mortal man

I'm locked away but still I sense
The pain that's felt beyond this fence

Out there the streets take lives each day
This game of death
      I wish not play
But may you REST IN PEACE my friend
Because one day we'll meet again

IN MEMORY OF ERIC MCGUIRE AKA TRICKY

UNTITLED 2

At night my life becomes a lonely soul
As if the shadow flourishes and persuades my wholesome days
To gently step into darkness
Never to unveil I am awaken by the nourishing smile of the sun,
Upward bound as the curtain of night is lifted and a new day begins

FOR TODAY WILL BE DIFFERENT
Those are my thoughts,
But the whispers of the midnight winds
And the miserable cries of the blue moon tell me that
Tonight is still the same
Tonight is still the same
Tonight is the night that I lay awake naked,
Wondering, when, for soon there's got to be a day,
Even if a brief and just for a moment
I will feel the breath of the idle evening,
Breathing at my spine
Only to be kissed by the lips of sanity
That usually seems to elude my view
Within the crevices of darkness
To be embraced by the face of the night time beast
That only seems to appear at the jab of my staff

And the heed of my call
I call no more
I cannot continue to call to this untamed creature of
Selfish turpitude only to be banished to the southern half of our world
A world that was once mine and shared by mystical entities
That came and went
Like the leaves of a tree when the seasons change
Never a moment when the leaves don't rustle
Unless my winds are contained
This tree of massive construction exists no more
But the leaves lie dormant on the foundation of my soul
As if they were to form a mattress left untouched
Untouched by seeming that the softest of caresses
Will only cause a crumble of my joy
YET, I must sleep

TO LOVE ME

To Love Me Is ...
    To know me completely
    To accept my good and my bad
    My wants, my needs
    My requests and desires
    To respect all of the struggles
    That I've had
TO LOVE ME IS ...
    To watch me grow
    To see my universe fully expand
    To wipe my tears, to fight my fears
    And help mold my transition into man
TO LOVE ME IS ...
    To remain at my side and to realize
    That you are my rib
    To accept my apologies, understand my ideologies
    And to forgive me for the things
    That I did
TO LOVE ME IS ...
    To seek truth in a world that's clouded by lies
    And congested with unclear visions
    But to find a reality in a real of spirituality
    And to stay focused as I make righteous decisions
TO LOVE ME IS ...

To continue as my friend
Through the pain, the rain
And the confusion
To never leave, to never deceive
To love me must be an illusion
To Love Me
Must Be……………………………..An ILLUSION

What is LIFE?

What is life without the things which are of immense importance?
What is love without a life to share it?
What is pleasure without the knowledge of pain?
      And without truth could one even bare it
What is the future to be foretold?
      If your past has all been in vain
What is a dream if reality's false or wicked?
What is victory if the taste is still sour?
      And defeat has entered right along with it

What is life?

THIS LOVE

Some love is not that, but an illusion
        And the conclusion is a mystical state
A falsified reality, where the dream of love bares weight
Yet, in real life, in my life, a good wife is a great,
        The ultimate mate
I won't say that destiny has gotten the best of me
        Because I think man determines his fate
And my choice is endless, eternal, forever
        However, the struggle is continually strong
Time and time you say you love music
        So consider this a love song

Some love is conforming, like the performing of an act
        That appears to be so real
While brothers envy the emotional longevity that we have created
        Most men would die to be Will
Not because I'm handsome
        For beauty is only in the beholder's view
Not because of my car, my rings, my things
        But the unending bond that I have with you

It's limitless, they mimic this
        They copy but always to no avail
This love is what I say love is
        And they all know that true love won't fail

Some loves perish, but cherish the thought
        Because you ought to know by now that this immortal love will just grow
Incessantly expanding throughout the cosmos
        And engulfing the universe whole
No limits exist when I speak of this,
        Because this love has an infinite range
One day your secret revealed that you were satisfied
        That classified our love as strange
Different, because most loves don't withstand
        Nor do lovers even try to make the bad days go away
But you've got me for life, my queen
This love
        Is here to stay

UNTITLED 3

Do you possibly understand that every day I live trying to make sure that I don't do anything to jeopardize our bond of sacred vowels and untainted love? Every day I anticipate that no matter what, it's going to be alright because we are in love. Then I have to think, can I speak for us or would it be to my best interest to speak for ME?

I am only able to speak for me, No one else. And would I really not want to speak for YOU, based on your actions. Well, lack of actions, and untamable reactions.

Rejection seems to be your brightest quality, and it's not fair. I feel as though 87%, or higher, of my days, as though you're in the other room sleeping on the floor. You are the most sexually selfish person that I have ever been involved with in my life. Yet, we are married. Do you realize that I have spent every night for 2 years and about 7 months, wanting to only be embraced by you?
JUST YOU!!!

Forever, is a long time to have a selfless love. At some point I must begin to love myself again, At least to feel loved by someone else.

THE ARROW OF CUPID

Dreaming by night and dreaming by day
    I hope we soon unite
The joy of love the pain of hate of which
    Shall win the fight
For joy is great and makes me laugh
    But also causes tears
The pain of hate is drawn away by the arrow
    Or cupid's spear
The arrow of cupid was shot towards I
    But seemed as though to miss
Till you I saw and felt I drawn to you
    I feel to kiss
But much too soon so till I wait
    And wait impatiently
For you to feel the arrows point
    And give your love to me
You see my eyes and witness the tear
    Yet it seems to remain so still
Cupid's wrath has sought to you
    But his arrow will never kill
So as we see as each has been struck
    The feeling to soon unite
The joy of love the pain of hate
    Of which shall win the fight

STUDIO PLAYER

A FRIEND ONCE ASKED DO YOU PLACE
GIRLS ON THE SHELF
AND I REPLIED NO WAY THEY CLIMB UP
THEMSELVES
THEN I HEARD A CRASH AND THE LEDGE
WAS NOT THERE
MY ID QUICKLY INFORMED ME I'M A
STUDIO PLAYER

IT SEEMS MY WHOLE EXISTENCE IS TO BE
TAUNTED AND TEMPTED
CAUSE ONCE I LEAVE THE CLUB SITE ALL
PLAYERISMS EXEMPTED
BUT WHEN I'M IN THAT REGION I'M
BOMBARDED WITH FREAKNICITY
WHEN ALL TO AVAIL AGAIN I FAIL, NO
AUTHENTICITY
IT'S ONLY FOR THAT MOMENT AND I MEAN
THAT MOMENT ALONE
IMMEDIATELY AFTER THAT LAST SONG
PLAYED
    I WIND UP ON THE SOLO CREEP TO
ONLY WANDER MY ASS BACK HOME
IS IT JUST ME AND MY G'S OR THAT ALL
BROADS ARE B'S
    OR THAT ME AND MY HOMEY JUST
GOT NO FLOWS
IS IT THAT OUR GAME IS LAME STUDIO
PLAYERS

I SUPPOSE ... OR IS IT THAT THE
VERY LAST STRAW
IS TO GIVE UP THE DRAWS
CAUSE THESE WOMEN ARE STUDIO
HOES

REAL EYES (REALIZE)

You don't realize that
    Beauty is the essence of your existence
    It is what, who, and why, you are
    And it shines with exquisite persistence
A star
    You are
    On a moonlight sky
    And
    You are the brightest, your glow is contagious
For you not to see
    Your possibilities
    Is
    Nothing less than outrageous
Confused a bit
    I'm assuming
    You do not understand your purpose
You're not
    Knowing that you're priceless
    At times showing that you feel worthless
When
    All the while your smile shows style
    And concern is a brand of its own
Even by yourself
    If you think of our hearts
    You will see that you can't be alone

You don't realize that
> Your existence is the essence of beauty
>> It is what, who, and why.
>>> Love is and will always flow fluently through me

MY NIGGA

What's up ... my nigga?
YO! That's my nigga!!!
    My nigga don't mean my slave
    It means a friend through thick and thin
    From the cradle to the grave
My nigga means my brotha
    My partner
    Part of the crew
My nigga could be anyone
    My nigga may be you
Though it's not a term for all to use
    I guess you'd understand
It's like saying what's up fool
    That doesn't mean a foolish man
    It means to me one cool ass dude
    Who's standing by my side
I think I could say I miss my nigga
    Since my Nigga Seekey died

REST IN PEACE ROBERT LEE SULLIVAN IV

MY ANGEL

My Angel doesn't sing so well
    My Angel doesn't fly
My Angel isn't sinless though,
    She'll do her best to try
She guards my heart with shield and sword
    Upon her soul I glide
She takes with her each and every part of myself
    That I can provide

My Angel is not yet perfect
    Though flawless by design
If I tell My Angel I have no wings
    Then she'll say borrow mine
Only an Angel would lend herself by your side
    For their entire life
My Angel stands eternal, My love,
    My Angel is my wife

MOTHER'S YEAR

I can't believe that we deceive
      Ourselves in such a way
It's so untrue to limit you
      To just one simple day
So now I'll grow and take time to show
      That I'm stating this so clear
That every day is MOTHER's DAY
      Let's call it MOTHER'S YEAR

MS. STRESS

STRESS
No more No less
Its wicked presence leaves an unbearable essence with a foul
Excuse me, flagrant foul, and demeanor
You see her?
Where about?
Not my crib, not where I live
Not where I reside
That bitch better hide
Or is it
Bitch better have my money
Fuck it, forget her, I don't have to live with her
Rather I'm poor or rich and if she did have my money then she wouldn't be a bitch
Not a bitch like a broad
Or a bitch like a dog
But a bitch like an issue
A sneeze with no tissue
A bitch with no skirt, but this bitch can sho flirt
Come real close to intimacy
But it's a kiss on the cheek
Getting our tinky winky to teletubby
Like a swinger Rick James freak
This magic moment was over quickly
Anyway, none the less
Life's a bitch then we die

So don't reply her name's stress
Life's a bitch then we die
So don't reply her name's stress
MS. STRESS if you're nasty

OR

Black is beautiful

Would you agree?
Is that why stare or gaze at me
Or is it insecurity
      Inferior to my kind
      Because we're gaining consciousness
      And strengthening our minds
Or do you stare because of hate
      You'd rather see me die
      Then live a life of worthiness, I'm waiting please reply
Or do you walk across the street
      When I walk down your side
      As if those who didn't cross the street that passed me must have died
Or is it that you wish to be like me deep down within
      You'd rather be my enemy since we cannot be kin
Or could it be you want my girl
      Though that I shall not give
      My Nubian queen is just for me and just for her I live
Or might it be the ability
      To play sports that I show
      We even have black quarterbacks and our skills still grow
Or do you dread the knowledge

>That I have and still receive
>My ancestors were scholars though
it may be hard to believe
All I ask is simple this
>I just want to know why
Instead of helping the human race
>You'd rather my race die

NO DEATH IN VAIN

Death ... is the orgasm of life
    It is when you come
    Come to an understanding or
    Overstanding of your essence and energy
    And its correlation with nature
Death consists of no flaws, no laws, and no guidelines
Its truth in itself, no red ink, or fine lines
Death is the fine print on your time spent
    A combination of escaping your flesh
    And being captured by the places your mind went
Life ... is death, cut and dry
You wonder why, sometimes, while others just wonder why not
You acquire your haven in the coolness of heaven
    While asking the negative, horny
    head what it's like being dead deep
    down under the hot spot
I suggest you make the best of the worst situation
I'm also inferring you turn your curse into blessings
Death is complete but not final,
    The departure and arrival

It's the memory of a freedom and a struggle called survival
It's to help you understand the plan
        So you fight the pain and maintain
Now it's our turn to live life to its fullest
And no death will be labeled in vain

ONE DAY

Take both combined, your heart and mind
    The truth shall override
If your bran and heart each play their part
    They both shall coincide
At some point they join to appoint the facts
    See true love is do or don't
It's not about control, it's about lettin' go
    Your soul can't decide will or won't
But the choice is not yours to conclude within
    It's whether or not you'll find true bliss without
And for some reason I hope, or should I say wish
    That these words will help you figure it out
But I've still got time
    And time will tell cause my patience still overflows
One Day you'll express that you love me
    And on that day
    I'll know

YOU WOULD THINK

    Yesterday, I was at the gym playing basketball with the same group of (white) guys that I've been playing with every Thursday for about 2 years. One of the guys and I were just having a general conversation about one of these guys (black) that played college football and almost got put off the team for walking out on an exam.

    The white guy looks at me and says, "And I think the class was African American studies, you would think that he knows that." Now, I know that he didn't mean anything intentionally racist by this, but, why would he be surprised that a black man, who in most of his growing years has never really learned African American history or even history (completely) didn't know African American studies.

    Would he be surprised if an American failed English? Of course not! Does he not realize that not all blacks know each other, nor do we all know that George Washington was a slave trader? We don't all know how blacks possess a stolen history, buried and burned by the white slave owners who would use extremely graphic means of inflicting terror on the slaves to make them (us) easier to control.

    We do not all know what went on and why slavery still exists and how affirmative action affects the nation. Then, the question is, is there a such thing as African American studies even though the essence of the African American is actually African. We should be studying the African, and his travels, and his struggles, as he evolved into the African American, as whitewashed as that story is. So, I guess the reply that I should have made is, "Do YOU know African American studies?" Or told the white guy; that the brother learned from the same school text books that he learned from.

African American studies would have had to have been taught at home, by parents who knew even less, and that they were taught by other slaves who had to sneak and read in the dark. I guess next time someone assumes that because you're an African in America, that you should know African American studies, I will say, NO, he shouldn't, he never learned our story, just HIStory.

www.ingramcontent.com/pod-product-compliance
Lightning Source LLC
Chambersburg PA
CBHW020653300426
44112CB00007B/359